Beautiful Classical Melodies for Solo Piano

CONTENTS

Arranged by John Nicholas, David Pearl, and Edwin McLean

Cherry Lane Music Company
Director of Publications/Project Editor: Mark Phillips
Publications Coordinator: Gabrielle Fastman

ISBN 978-1-57560-719-1

Visit our website at www.cherrylane.com

Air on the G String

from ORCHESTRAL SUITE NO. 3

By Johann Sebastian Bach

Slowly

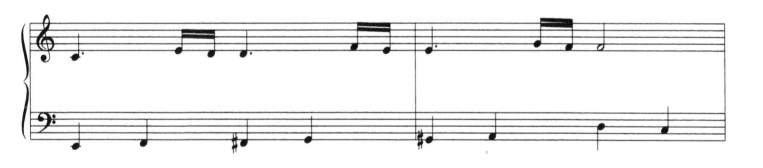

Ave Maria

By Franz Schubert

Moderately slow

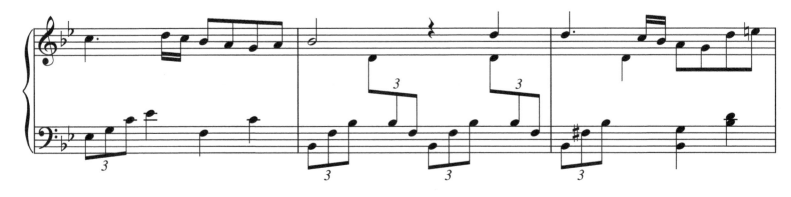

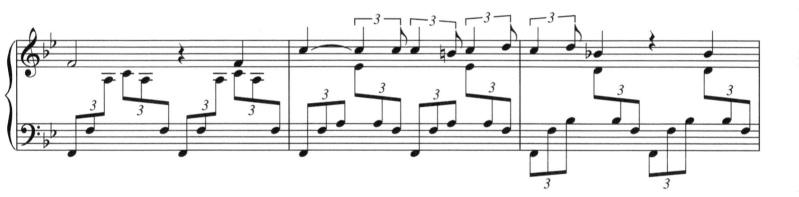

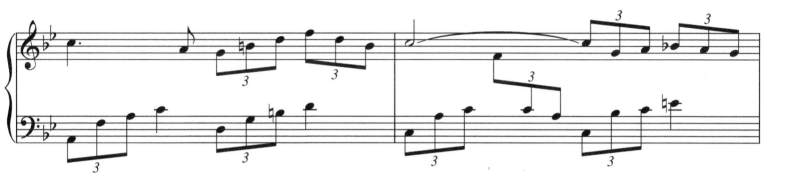

Ave Verum Corpus

(Jesu, Word of God Incarnate)

By Wolfgang Amadeus Mozart

Moderately slow

rit.

Be Thou with Me

By Johann Sebastian Bach

Moderately slow

mp

rit.

Canon in D

Andante

By Johann Pachelbel

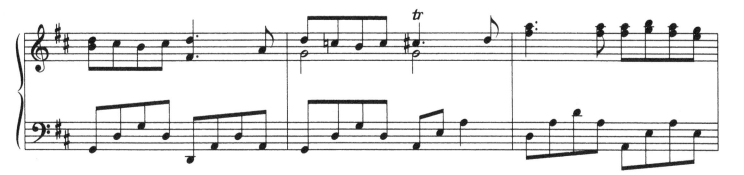

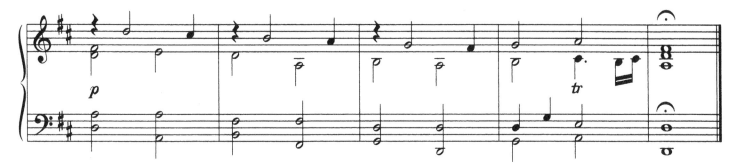

Cantique de Jean Racine

By Gabriel Fauré

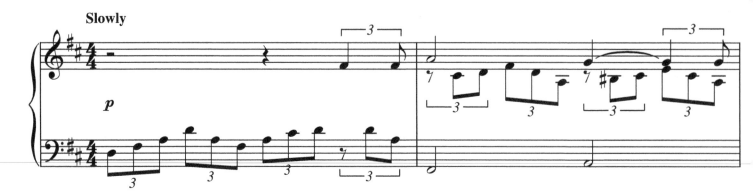

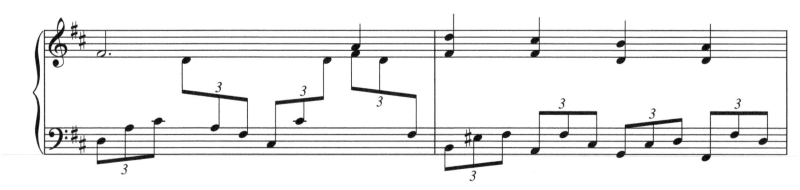

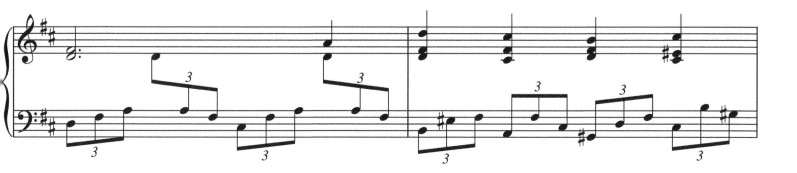

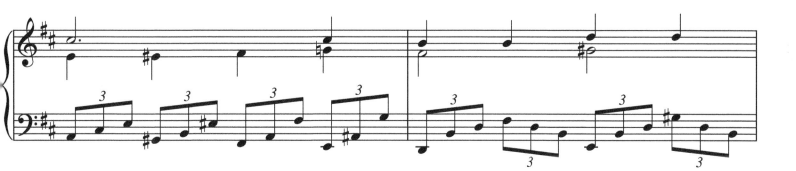

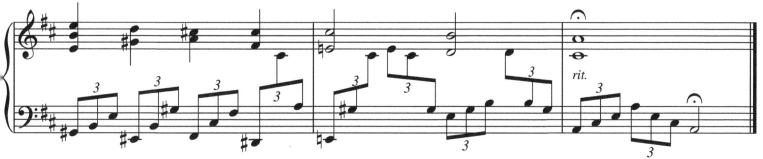

Caro mio ben

Music by Tommaso Giordani

Moderately slow

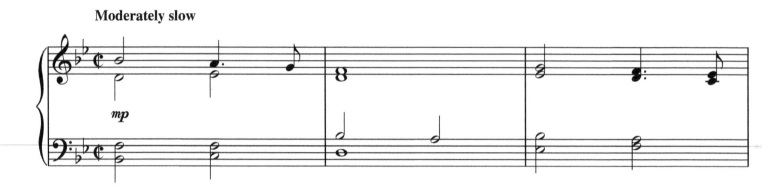

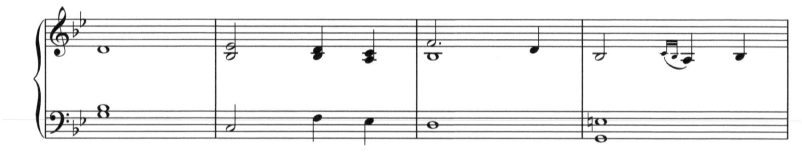

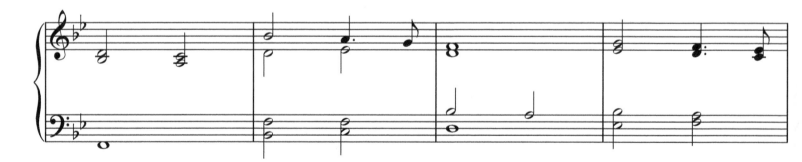

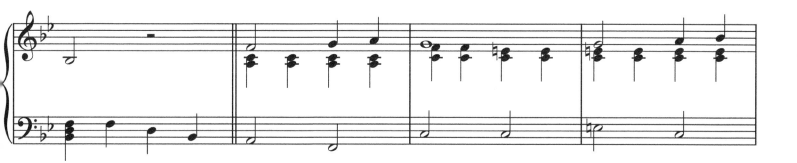

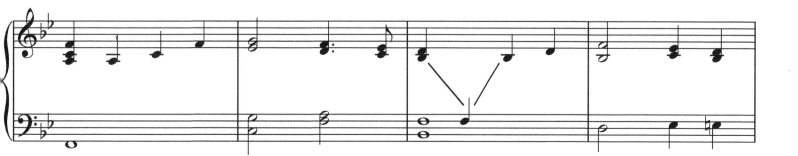

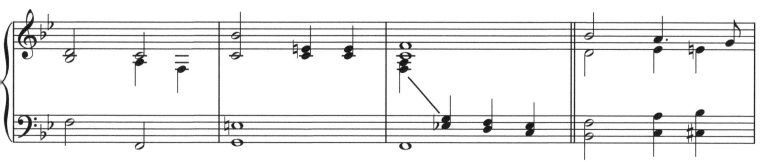

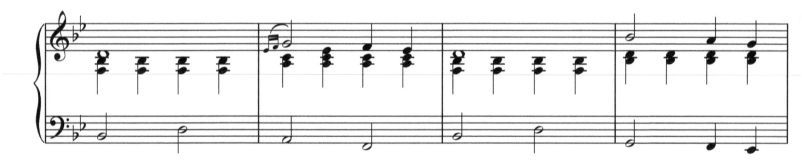

Slowly   **Tempo I**

Intermezzo
from CAVALLERIA RUSTICANA

By Pietro Mascagni

Slowly

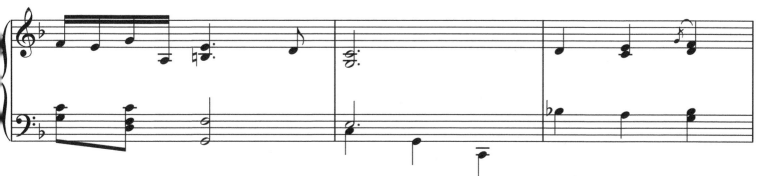

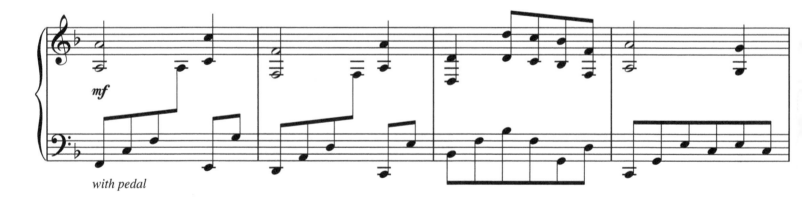

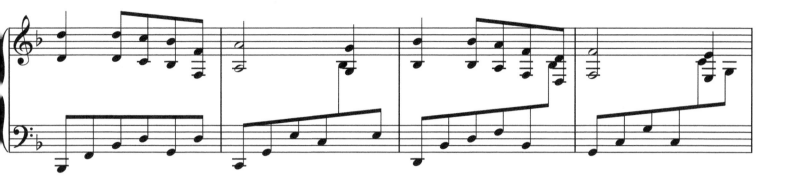

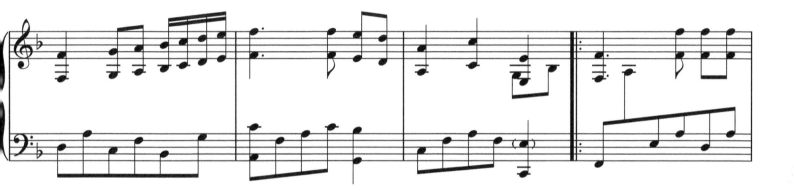

rit. e dim.

p

Jerusalem

By Hubert Parry

Moderately

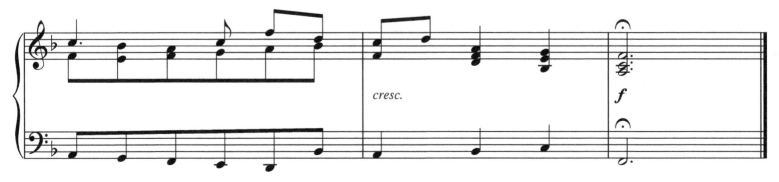

cresc.

f

Jesu, Joy of Man's Desiring

By Johann Sebastian Bach

Andante cantabile

Laudate Dominum

from VESPERAE SOLENNES

By Wolfgang Amadeus Mozart

Slowly, in 1

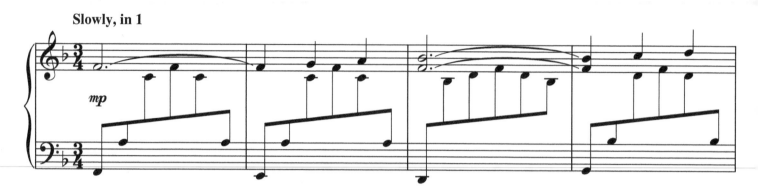

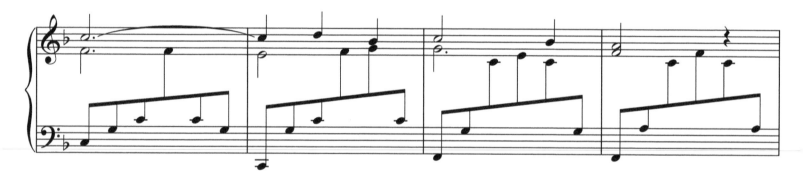

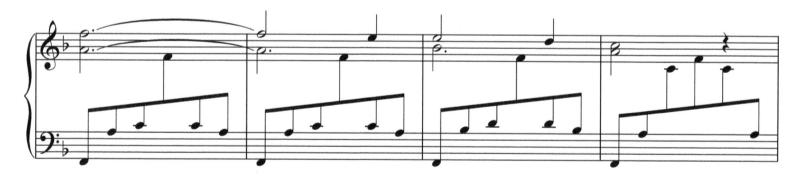

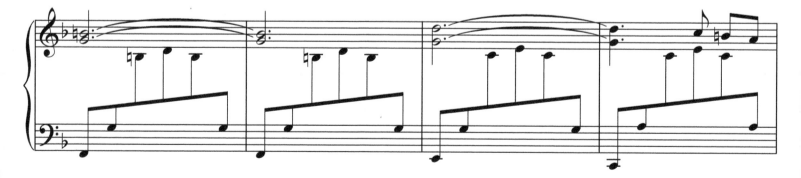

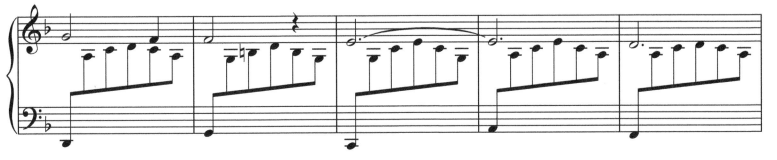

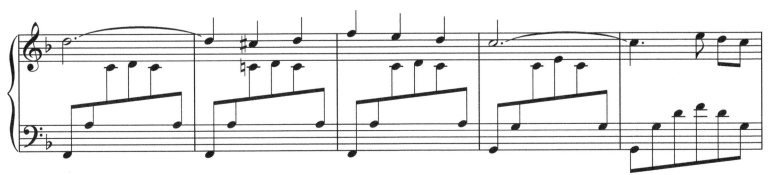

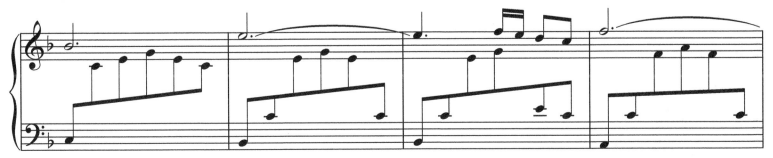

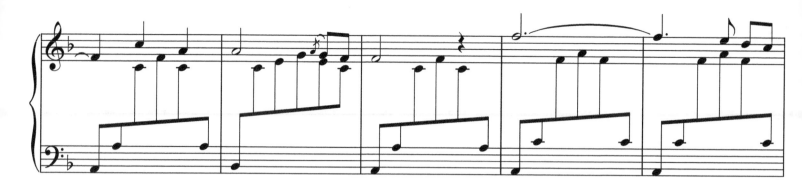

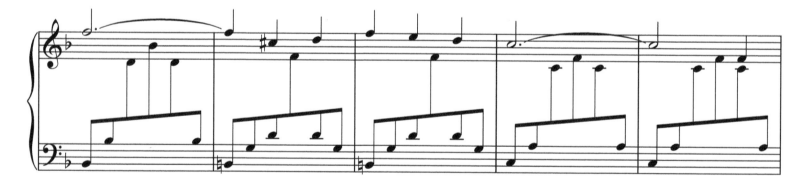

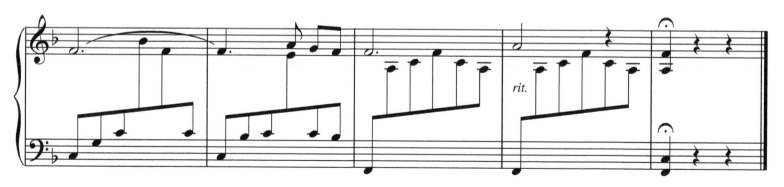

Pavane

By Gabriel Fauré

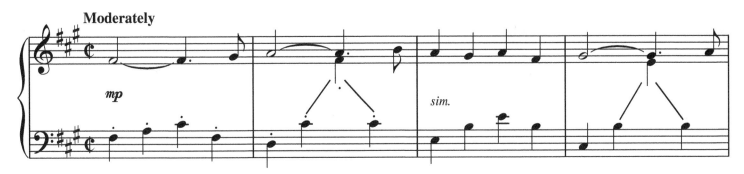

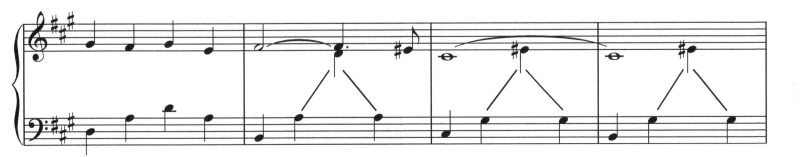

To Coda ✛

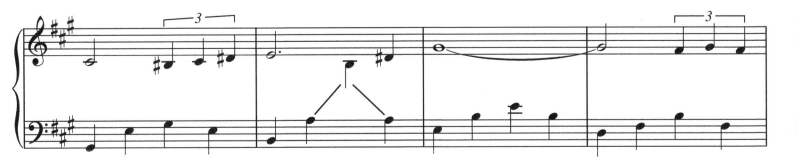

D.C. al Coda

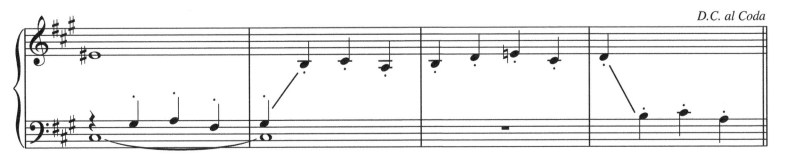

Coda

rit.

O mio babbino caro

from GIANNI SCHICCHI

By Giacomo Puccini

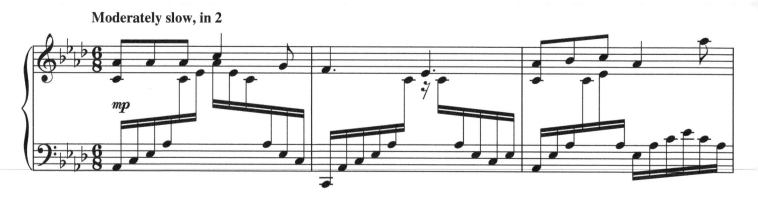

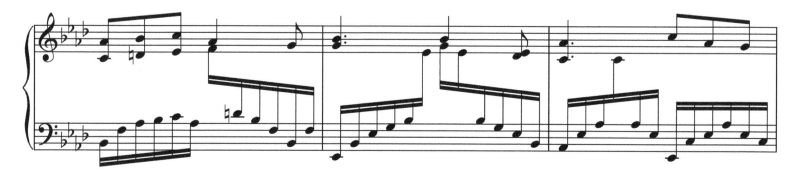

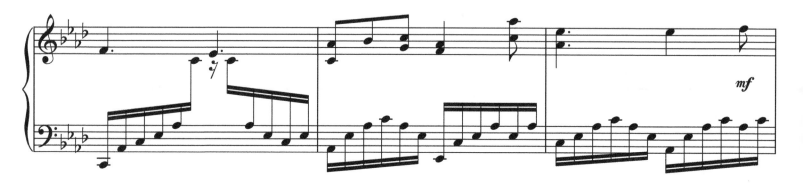

Panis Angelicus
(O Lord Most Holy)

By César Franck

Moderately slow

mp

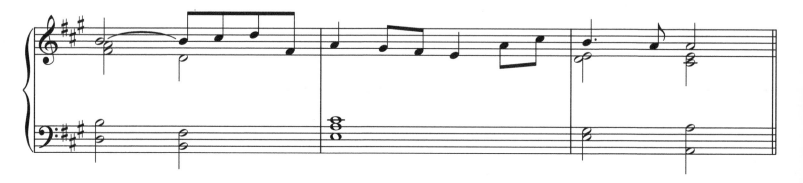

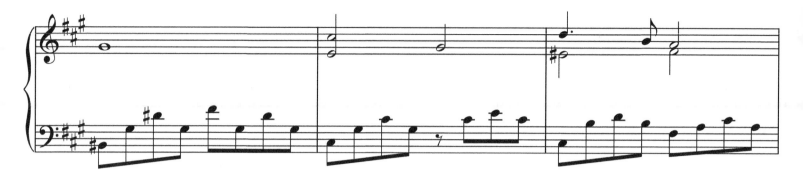

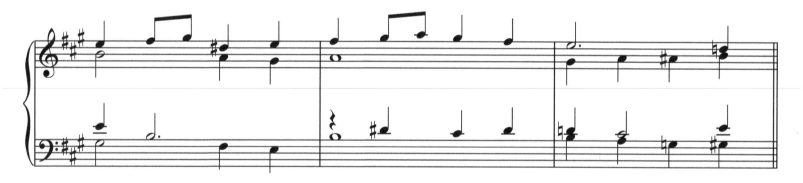

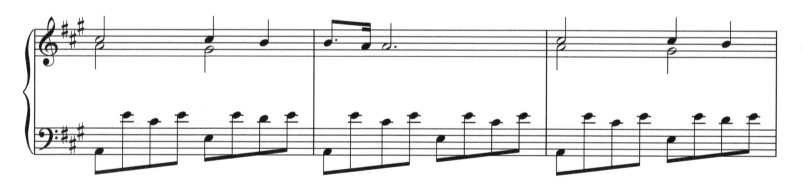

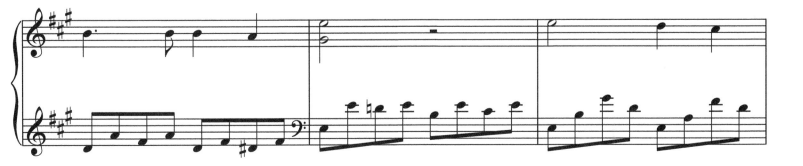

Pavane for a Dead Princess

By Maurice Ravel

Moderately slow

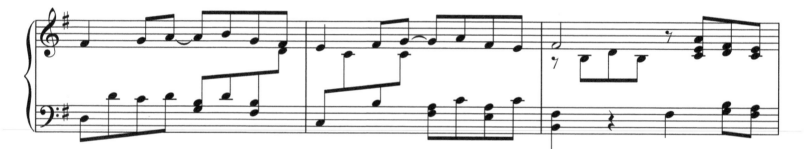

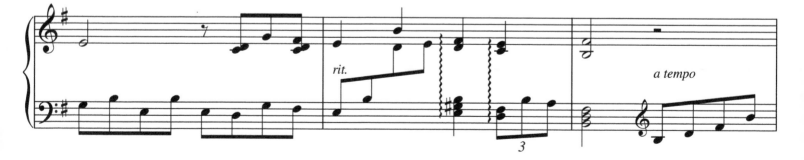

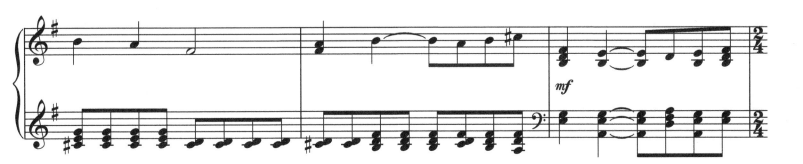

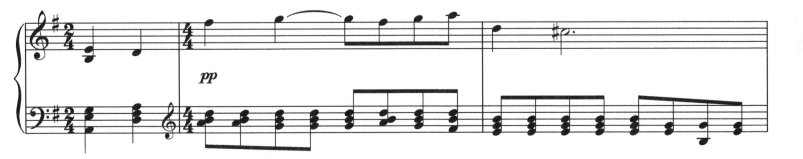

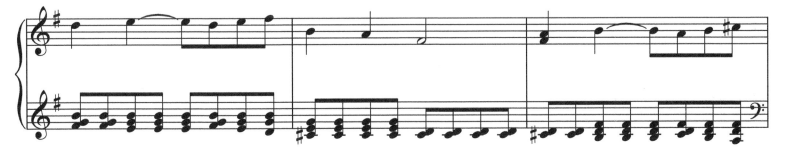

Piano Concerto in F Minor
(Second Movement)

By Johann Sebastian Bach

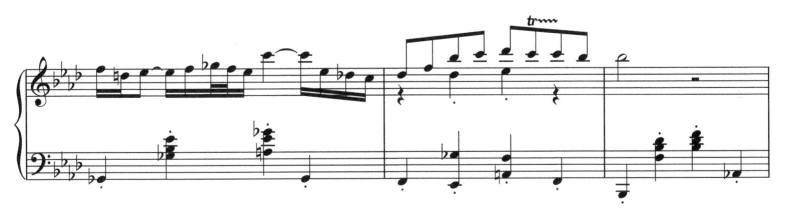

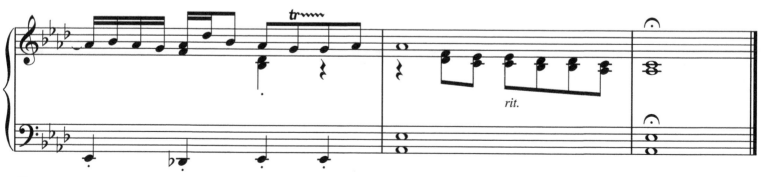

Pie Jesu
from REQUIEM

By Gabriel Fauré

Moderately slow

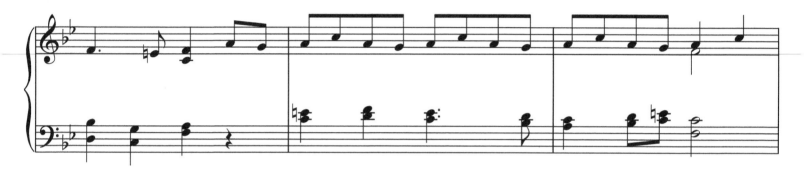

rit.

Sheep May Safely Graze

from CANTATA NO. 208

By Johann Sebastian Bach

Symphony No. 3

Third Movement

By Johannes Brahms

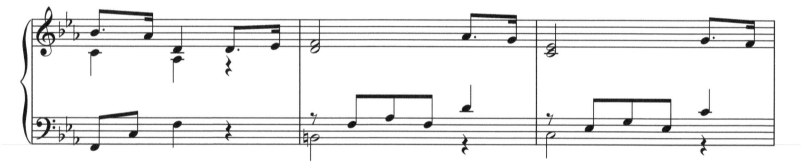

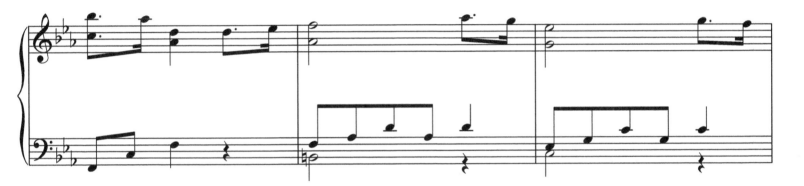

Symphony No. 5

Second Movement

By Franz Schubert

Moderately

More Great Piano/Vocal Books

FROM CHERRY LANE

For a complete listing of Cherry Lane titles available,
including contents listings, please visit our web site at
www.cherrylane.com

02501590	Sara Bareilles – Kaleidoscope Heart $17.99
02501136	Sara Bareilles – Little Voice $16.95
00102353	Sara Bareilles – Once Upon Another Time $12.99
02501505	The Black Eyed Peas – The E.N.D. . $19.99
02502171	The Best of Boston $17.95
02501614	Zac Brown Band – The Foundation $19.99
02501618	Zac Brown Band – You Get What You Give $19.99
02501123	Buffy the Vampire Slayer – Once More with Feeling $18.95
02500665	Sammy Cahn Songbook $24.95
02501688	Colbie Caillat – All of You $17.99
02501454	Colbie Caillat – Breakthrough $17.99
02501127	Colbie Caillat – Coco $16.95
02500838	Best of Joe Cocker $16.95
02502165	John Denver Anthology – Revised. . $22.95
02500002	John Denver Christmas $14.95
02502166	John Denver's Greatest Hits $17.95
02502151	John Denver – A Legacy in Song (Softcover) $24.95
02500566	Poems, Prayers and Promises: The Art and Soul of John Denver $19.95
02500326	John Denver – The Wildlife Concert $17.95
02500501	John Denver and the Muppets: A Christmas Together $9.95
02501186	The Dresden Dolls – The Virginia Companion $39.95
02509922	The Songs of Bob Dylan $29.95
02500497	Linda Eder – Gold $14.95
02500396	Linda Eder – Christmas Stays the Same. $17.95
02502209	Linda Eder – It's Time $17.95
02501542	Foreigner – The Collection $19.99
02500535	Erroll Garner Anthology. $19.95
02500318	Gladiator $12.95
02502126	Best of Guns N' Roses $17.95
02502072	Guns N' Roses – Selections from Use Your Illusion I and II $17.95
02500014	Sir Roland Hanna Collection $19.95
02501447	Eric Hutchinson – Sounds Like This $17.99
02500856	Jack Johnson – Anthology $19.95
02501140	Jack Johnson – Sleep Through the Static $16.95

02501564	Jack Johnson – To the Sea $19.99
02501546	Jack's Mannequin – *The Glass Passenger* and *The Dear Jack EP* $19.99
02500834	The Best of Rickie Lee Jones $16.95
02500381	Lenny Kravitz – Greatest Hits $14.95
02501318	John Legend – Evolver. $19.99
02500822	John Legend – Get Lifted $16.99
02503701	Man of La Mancha $11.95
02501047	Dave Matthews Band – Anthology. . $24.95
02502192	Dave Matthews Band – Under the Table and Dreaming . . . $17.95
02501514	John Mayer Anthology – Volume 1 . . . . $22.99
02501504	John Mayer – Battle Studies. $19.99
02500987	John Mayer – Continuum. $16.95
02500681	John Mayer – Heavier Things. $16.95
02500563	John Mayer – Room for Squares . . $16.95
02500081	Natalie Merchant – Ophelia $14.95
02502446	Jason Mraz – Love Is a Four Letter Word $19.99
02500863	Jason Mraz – Mr. A-Z. $17.95
02501467	Jason Mraz – We Sing. We Dance. We Steal Things. . $19.99
02502895	Nine $17.95
02501411	Nine – Film Selections $19.99
02500425	Time and Love: The Art and Soul of Laura Nyro $21.99
02502204	The Best of Metallica $17.95
02501497	Ingrid Michaelson – Everybody . . . $17.99
02501496	Ingrid Michaelson – Girls and Boys $19.99
02501768	Ingrid Michaelson – Human Again . $17.99
02501529	Monte Montgomery Collection. . . . $24.99
02500857	Anna Nalick – Wreck of the Day . . $16.95
02501336	Amanda Palmer – Who Killed Amanda Palmer? $17.99
02501004	Best of Gram Parsons $16.95
02500010	Tom Paxton – The Honor of Your Company $17.95
02507962	Peter, Paul & Mary – Holiday Concert. $17.95
02500145	Pokemon 2.B.A. Master $12.95
02500026	The Prince of Egypt $16.95
02500660	Best of Bonnie Raitt $17.95
02502189	The Bonnie Raitt Collection $22.95
02502088	Bonnie Raitt – Luck of the Draw . . $14.95
02507958	Bonnie Raitt – Nick of Time. $14.95
02502218	Kenny Rogers – The Gift $16.95
02501577	She & Him – Volume One $16.99

02501578	She & Him – Volume Two $16.99
02500414	Shrek. $16.99
02500536	Spirit – Stallion of the Cimarron . . . $16.95
02500166	Steely Dan – Anthology $17.95
02500622	Steely Dan – Everything Must Go. . . $14.95
02500284	Steely Dan – Two Against Nature . . . $14.95
02500344	Billy Strayhorn: An American Master $17.95
02500515	Barbra Streisand – Christmas Memories $16.95
02502164	Barbra Streisand – The Concert. . $22.95
02500550	Essential Barbra Streisand $24.95
02502228	Barbra Streisand – Higher Ground $17.99
02501065	Barbra Streisand – Live in Concert 2006 . . . . $19.95
02501485	Barbra Streisand – Love Is the Answer. $19.99
02501722	Barbra Streisand – What Matters Most $19.99
02502178	The John Tesh Collection $17.95
02503623	John Tesh – A Family Christmas. . . $15.95
02503630	John Tesh – Grand Passion $16.95
02500307	John Tesh – Pure Movies 2 . . . . $16.95
02501068	The Evolution of Robin Thicke. . . . $19.95
02500565	Thoroughly Modern Millie. $17.99
02501399	Best of Toto $19.99
02502175	Tower of Power – Silver Anniversary $17.95
02501403	Keith Urban – Defying Gravity $17.99
02501008	Keith Urban – Love, Pain & The Whole Crazy Thing $17.95
02501141	Keith Urban – Greatest Hits $16.99
02502198	The "Weird Al" Yankovic Anthology. $17.95
02500334	Maury Yeston – December Songs. . $17.95
02502225	The Maury Yeston Songbook $19.95

See your local music dealer or contact:

EXCLUSIVELY DISTRIBUTED BY
HAL•LEONARD® CORPORATION
7777 W. BLUEMOUND RD. P.O. BOX 13819 MILWAUKEE, WI 53213

Prices, contents and availability subject to change without notice.

1112